Praise for *Be a Dog with a Bone*

"A genuine masterpiece that reveals the true secrets to wisdom, success, and fulfillment from the creatures who are most qualified to teach them to us . . . dogs."

— **Paul Hartunian**, publicity expert

"I love it! It's charming and wise, playful and brilliant, easy yet profound."

— **Joe Vitale**, the #1 best-selling author of *Spiritual Marketing*

"This insightful book cleverly delivers a profound yet meaningful approach on how you can turn your deepest desires into reality and transform your life."

— **Mark Victor Hansen**, the co-creator of the #1 *New York Times* best-selling series *Chicken Soup for the Soul* and the co-author of *The One Minute Millionaire*

"Peggy's book offers fun and positive insights into the power of animals to teach us and enrich our lives. Her 'doggy' lessons instruct about serious life changes, while her stories and cartoons bring smiles, reminding us of the antics of our own four-footed family members."

— **Linda M. Hines**, the former president and CEO of Delta Society

"This book is sure to be a classic. It's fast . . . it's simple . . . it works! Peggy McColl will show you precisely what to do to hold on to your dreams <u>and</u> to turn them into reality!"

— **Bob Proctor**, the best-selling author of *You Were Born Rich*

*"My nine dogs and I found inspiration and fun with **Be a Dog with a Bone**. Each of them thinks Peggy is referring to them. I know she is referring to me."*

— **Patty Duke**, actress and author

Be a Dog with a Bone

Be a Dog
with a Bone

Always Go for Your Dreams

Peggy McColl

HAY HOUSE, INC.
Carlsbad, California • New York City
London • Sydney • Johannesburg
Vancouver • Hong Kong • New Delhi

Published and distributed in the United States by: Hay House, Inc.: www.hayhouse.com • *Published and distributed in Australia by:* Hay House Australia Pty. Ltd.: www.hayhouse.com.au • *Published and distributed in the United Kingdom by:* Hay House UK, Ltd.: www.hayhouse.co.uk • *Published and distributed in the Republic of South Africa by:* Hay House SA (Pty), Ltd.: www.hayhouse.co.za • *Distributed in Canada by:* Raincoast: www.raincoast.com • *Published in India by:* Hay House Publishers India: www.hayhouse.co.in

Editorial supervision: Jill Kramer • *Design:* Tricia Breidenthal
Cartoons provided by: Randy Glasbergen

A previous edition of this book was published in book and e-book form by Destinies Publishing in 2003. **ISBN:** 0-9730431-1-3

Library of Congress Cataloging-in-Publication Data

McColl, Peggy.
  Be a dog with a bone : always go for your dreams / Peggy McColl. -- 1st ed.
    p. cm.
  ISBN 978-1-4019-2464-5 (hardcover : alk. paper) 1. Self-actualization (Psychology) 2. Success--Psychological aspects.. 3. Dreams. 4. Dogs--Miscellanea. I. Title.
  BF637.S4M234 2009
  158.1--dc22

                              2008038179

ISBN: 978-1-4019-2464-5

12 11 10 09   4 3 2 1
1st edition, January 2009

*To my sister, Judy, who reminds me
to always go for my dreams.*

Contents

Foreword

You never know how tough you are until someone takes your bone away!

Leave it to a bulldog—me—to write the Foreword to Peggy McColl's book *Be a Dog with a Bone*. After all, we bulldogs are bred to have dogged determination. It's in our genes. Have you ever noticed how our noses are slanted backward so that we can breathe without letting go of that bone?

In these pages, Peggy McColl explains how you can follow some doggone good guidelines not only to succeed but also to simplify your life. As a matter of fact, I wish I'd read her work a few years back when I was starting my business, Zelda Wisdom. I chased my tail, I ingested things that weren't good for me, and I spent a lot of time in the doghouse. Life is "ruff," and barking up the wrong trees instead of using my instincts to reach my goals didn't help. Once I found my "bone," however, success came quickly.

Be a Dog with a Bone briefly defines how you can learn some helpful tricks from humans' best friends. I especially liked Peggy's concept of "drool unto others as you would have them drool unto you." I keep that message posted above my dog bowl.

The book will keep you thinking and smiling at the same time. Best of all, it will teach you the tricks you need to reach your goals, follow your dreams, and succeed when you don't think you can. Success comes when you can hang on after others let go. So *go for it!*

— **Zelda the Dog**
(www.zeldawisdom.com)

Introduction

If I think about my own life and what has allowed me to get through challenging times, overcome obstacles, stay focused on my deepest desires, and achieve my goals, it all comes down to the sheer power of determination. If I think about those who have inspired me—and thousands, or even *millions,* of others—they too had dogged determination. Whatever their dreams, they held on to them like a dog with a bone.

Allow me to be very clear from the outset: to be a dog with a bone does not involve growling, biting, snapping, barking, or mistreating any other human being. Nor does it mean that you're supposed to be needy, jealous, boastful, envious, or inflexible; forget about what's most important to you; or lose sight of your values. Dogged determination means holding on to that which you most value, as well as working in a positive way to make your dreams come true.

Being a dog with a bone is *not* an unhealthy attachment. You aren't obsessed with your goal; rather, you have a clear intent to achieve it. Attachment is unhealthy because it causes you to close yourself off from possibilities. Intention means that you have a strong desire, but if you don't achieve your goal, you can accept that. I believe Deepak Chopra spoke well when he recommended that everyone should be "attached to nothing and open to everything."

As a matter of fact, most determined people don't actually know how they're going to attain their dreams. They don't become attached to how the universe will answer their intent—they simply decide what they want, grab it, and hold on tightly, having faith that the "how" will reveal itself in time.

It is my intention to share with you my vision of being a dog with a bone in order to help you realize your own dreams. I use dog metaphors because these animals represent beautiful, admirable, and desirable goal-achieving qualities such as persistence, playfulness, loyalty, and unconditional love. So to be a dog with a bone means that you're someone who wants to achieve a specific outcome and remain steadfast in the pursuit of that goal, overcoming roadblocks, refusing to give up, and maintaining unwavering faith. All you have to do to become such an individual is decide what you want and then turn on a dormant, powerful, positive emotion inside of you that can be set into action to propel you forward. In other words, you must learn how to use your intention to create that which you desire. Isn't that what life is all about? You bet it is!

What Is Your Bone?

Each of us has a desire to discover the great secrets of success, experience total contentment, and find the path to personal fulfillment. For centuries, we've turned to wise men and women for guidance: we've climbed to the hermit's highest cave, trekked through the desert to meet the sage, and scoured the self-help section in bookstores for hours on end in our search for answers. But after all this time, is it possible that we may have been looking in the wrong places?

All around you there are reminders about how to achieve success . . . you just happen to be overlooking them. As the saying goes, "Success leaves clues." But don't look up, out, or in—look down! All the inspiration and insight you need might just be curled up at your feet.

In all seriousness, we humans can learn from our canine friends who enjoy happy, stress-free lives. Imagine what kind of world we'd live in if we all shared the same high level of commitment, determination, playfulness, unconditional love, and true loyalty that dogs do. Imagine if we all trusted and followed our instincts. Imagine if we all reveled in the simple pleasures of life: running freely in an open field; driving down the country road with our head stuck out the window and the wind blowing through our hair; accepting the warm invitation to take a walk with a friend; or playing happily for hours, never showing signs of fatigue. We have a lot to learn from our wise four-legged friends.

So are you feeling restless and unsatisfied? Have you given up on a dream you once had? Is there something you deeply desire, something you'd like to grab hold of and never let go? Are you ready to trust in the universe and courageously step out, one paw at a time? If you answered yes to these questions, then *Be a Dog with a Bone* is definitely for you.

I hope that as you read this book, you're inspired to discover passion, persistence, devotion, and joyfulness; and that success will naturally follow as you hold on to your intent. (As you're reading, dog-ear the pages that have significant value for you so that you can return to them later for inspiration and future reference.) You may be pleasantly surprised to find out how simple goal achieving really is.

Grab on and hold tight to your dream as you reconnect to what's important to you and capture the essence of one of the most powerful keys to success: dogged determination. Come for a journey with me in which we'll dig up your dreams, sniff out your strengths, and roll in the bliss of success!

— **Peggy McColl**

Chapter 1

Dogged Determination

Grab hold of that bone and never let it go!

. . . .

> *"Get a good idea and stay with it. Dog it,*
> *and work it until it's done and done right."*
> — Walt Disney

Have you ever witnessed a dog with a bone? No matter how hard you try to wrench it out of that pooch's mouth, she won't let go. As a matter of fact, the more you attempt to take the bone away, the deeper the dog will sink her teeth in. That is sheer, dogged determination, a quality that is absolutely required if you want to achieve any goal, no matter how large or small—that is, regardless of the size of the bone.

1

The late Maurice Richard was a dog with a bone when it came to pursuing his dream of playing hockey. It was very clear what he wanted to do with his life early on, even though he incurred a large number of injuries at a young age. While he was ultimately accepted to play with the Montreal Canadiens, very early in his career he was labeled a "frail" player. He was also challenged by a lack of support from those around him, except for his devoted wife. Maurice's passion for the sport took him past these obstacles, however, and led him to a record-breaking career of more than 20 years. He had a bone and would not let go!

When *you* know what you want, and you have no doubt that you want it, you need to become just like Maurice Richard. Clench your teeth firmly on your bone and don't let it go. Be determined not to allow anyone or anything to take it from you.

Many circumstances can make it difficult to hold on, such as health challenges or your own doubts and fears. Other people, even well-meaning loved ones, may also try to yank that bone away from you. When you face these obstacles, you just need to turn up the volume on your determination and feel the passion of your desire, the force that will propel you toward your goals.

While being determined is crucial, it's also important to open yourself up to receive new ideas and expand your thinking. You must be ready to let go of those limiting thoughts that feature the words *should* and *ought,* such as, *I should be realistic and not make such a lofty goal for myself,* or *I ought to do what the people I love want me to do instead of pursuing my own passion.* Go for what you really want!

Challenge yourself to scratch out a new path and chase your dream, but be careful of the route you take. Be willing to explore new paths; after all, if you travel the same route that you've been taking thus far, you'll end up at the same destination. Is that where you long to go?

What Is Your Bone?

Before you read any further, think about the following questions: *Do you know what you want? Do you have a dream that you wish would come true or a goal you want to achieve, one that you're truly passionate about?* Don't turn more one page of this work until you've connected to your deepest desire, your biggest dream. What is it?

If you could have anything, and I mean *anything,* what would it be? Write it down, and as you go through this book, keep your dream in mind. In these pages, you'll find out how to make that dream a reality.

Here are a few guidelines for writing down your goal:

1. Be clear about what you want, and if you know the specifics, include those.

2. Use only positive words.

3. Write your goal in the present tense, as if you've already achieved it.

The following are some examples of goals:

— I am achieving to the point that I'm going beyond my sales objectives. My clients are thrilled with the service I'm delivering, and my company is ecstatic with the numbers I'm doing. I am a true achiever, and it shows.

— I am a straight-A student and excelling in school. I put my heart and soul into my work and enjoy the many benefits of being a top scholar. I feel really good about myself. And I am inspiring others to excel in education as well.

— *I am completing a full marathon in record time, feeling exhilarated, accomplished, and ready to take on the world. I am in the best physical condition of my life, and I look and feel great!*

— *I have a successful, profitable, honest, growing business with ecstatic customers and joyful and capable employees. I work in my business 30 hours a week or less. My revenues exceed a million dollars, and my profit is at an all-time high.*

— *I am a loving, healthy, honest, warm, kind, considerate, romantic, sweet, playful, confident wife who is loved in return. My relationship with my husband is absolutely wonderful. We are both very happy with each other and completely committed to our relationship. We live in marital bliss.*

— *I enjoy being a member of a winning team in the National Hockey League. I am setting new goal-scoring records and inspiring others to go for their dreams. I am demonstrating the absolute best of myself each and every day, on and off the ice.*

— *I own outright a stunning, solidly built, professionally decorated, beautifully landscaped, first-class, quality four-bedroom, five-bathroom, 5,000-square-foot house with a three-car garage on a spectacular lot! My family is safe at all times in our home, and we all love living here.*

— I am a New York Times best-selling author. I am known throughout the world in a very positive way, as well as being highly respected in my business. My work is making a positive and beneficial contribution to the lives of millions of others.

Now write down your own deepest desire in a notebook or on a sheet of paper.

Even if you haven't met your goal yet, be sure to speak about it as if you've already accomplished it. As you read your deepest desire aloud, create in yourself the emotions you'd feel if it were 100 percent true right now. As you do, you'll notice the excitement building in you. That feeling is your passion, and it's the force that ignites your determination to pursue your goals. Passion will keep your jaws clenched on your bone and stop you from letting it slip away or be taken from you.

If your dream doesn't come from desire or passion, it's less likely that you'll maintain a high level of tenacity. You may have wondered why you haven't been able to stick to a goal—well, maybe you need to take a look at whether it's truly something that you're excited about. If you are, great! Just ignite that spark once again and keep it going. If not, ask yourself why you feel you have to pursue that aim. Isn't there some other goal you've been ignoring that makes you feel the power of your passion? If so, acknowledge it and pursue it!

Desires, Dreams, and Determination

Dreams are not always obvious. So if you think that someone is going to deliver a wonderful dream to you, all wrapped up in a pretty bow, think again. You've got to be willing to sniff out that bone, just as dogs do—they'll dig in many different places until they find the treasure that they know is there. Your goals and desires may be out there (undiscovered, or not yet uncovered) or in there, inside your heart, waiting for you to find them. From time to time, your bone may show up and you'll know exactly what you want to do with your life. But if you don't have a clear vision, you'll need to dig some more . . . don't stop until you uncover that dream.

Keep in mind that sometimes you may mistake short-lived wants for dreams. A short-lived want is often the result of a "be nice to have" thought. In other words, while it would be nice to have a new car, let's say, your desire to obtain it might not stay all that strong if you don't really need it.

A deep desire, on the other hand, comes from the soul, and you'll recognize it simply by the way you feel about it in your heart. When you uncover this bone, you'll have deep determination, because determination is fueled by desire. Short-lived wants don't run deep, and there's nothing wrong with that. But it's vitally important to connect with the deepest dream of your heart, for when you do, you'll access your dogged determination.

When you have this type of determination, you feel an abundance of energy flowing through your body, which comes with a lot of excitement. Your ability to focus is then intensified: you set your sights on a target and don't allow anything to distract you, no matter what happens.

Dogged determination means that you're holding on to your dream more tightly than ever. If someone tries to pry this dream away from you, it isn't going to happen. You take action toward its attainment every day, and even if you don't know how you'll achieve your goal, you keep going. When a challenge comes along, you get excited because you know that this is an opportunity to reveal the best of who you are, which is exactly what challenges are designed to do.

When you have such determination, you know that nothing is going to stop you. You become more energized, committed, and persistent every day. You exude confidence, knowing for certain that you'll achieve your goal because there's no other possible outcome. Being determined gives you an incredible natural high. You know that nothing will stop you, and you show it in everything you do.

Yet being determined doesn't mean being without fear. You may feel afraid, but you'll move forward, take action, and be completely optimistic anyway.

The following formula summarizes this well: desire + focus + courage = determination.

What We Can Learn from Max

David Booth's dog, Max, is very determined to play. As David explains:

Our Scottish terrier, Max—born Maximilian McDuff—is incorrigible. He loves to play; he loves everybody and everything. If you start playing fetch with him, he will keep going and going. Max's playfulness and persistence know no limits. If you're sitting down, he'll keep bringing you the ball and begging for you to throw it.

When we have a guest over, Max knows that he has a new mark. He'll go over and drop his toy at our guest's feet and will keep doing it until he or she picks it up and throws it. Our Scottie simply doesn't quit—he'll keep at it until he gets his way.

Max probably removed the word *stop* from his "recognition vocabulary," as dog trainers would say. (Although if he did hear it, he probably wouldn't listen anyway.) Because of his determination, he achieves what he desires.

I've noticed human beings behaving the same way, particularly salespeople who won't be deterred. Even when you say, "No, thank you!" they keep selling. It's almost as if they don't hear the words. And if they keep asking in a style that isn't offensive, or they come back later to try again and again, they're likely to get the result they're striving for.

Max reminds us to keep going and remain cute and playful. He's not intrusive or obnoxious—he simply has a desire to play, and he asks you to play with him. Sooner or later, this little Scottie achieves the result he intended. That's the power of dogged determination.

When you expand your thoughts from being just a dog with a desire to play to someone who is *determined* to play, you can achieve great goals. You can go from being a ballplayer who merely enjoys the game to a world-champion athlete, or from a reliable and pleasant worker to a highly successful and enthusiastic businessperson. The key ingredient in this transformation is determination, also known as stick-to-itiveness, tenacity, or perseverance. Certainly, world-champion athletes and successful businesspeople have their share of challenges, but even so, they maintain their determination. In the face of adversity, they put themselves right back on track again.

Discovering Your Determination

Your own determination may be a sleeping dog, lying dormant inside of you. If it's unexpressed, you may have no drive, focus, or direction for your life . . . but it's still there. You can think of determination as energy stored within you. You have the ability to flip the switch and turn it on, and you have the ability to turn it off, too. Which do you choose?

Erin Brockovich, immortalized by Julia Roberts in the movie based on her life, was a single mom with no ambitions or goals for herself. After her attorney couldn't negotiate a settlement from a car accident she was in, she insisted that he hire her, since she was out of cash and out of work. Her lawyer was so impressed by her tenacity that he indeed employed her, and while on the job, Erin found a cause that inspired her passion. She discovered that a power company had been covering up the fact that they'd polluted the local water supply, creating illness and disease in the community. Erin doggedly pursued her goal of suing the company to force them to clean up the toxins—and along the way, she discovered her own capacity, talent, and passion for achieving justice for people harmed by uncaring corporations.

Just like Erin, we all have a unique set of talents and deep desires that we can use to make a difference in the lives of ourselves and others, but we won't find those bones unless we take action and start sniffing for them.

Hold on to Your Values

I'd like to take a moment here to stress that while you need determination as you move toward your goal, it's equally important to keep in sight your most important values: health, honesty, integrity, family, friends, finances, and so on. Being a dog with a bone doesn't mean that you take leave of your senses or lose your priorities. On the contrary—when you're pursuing a goal, it's more important than ever to use your keen sense of logic, engage your common sense, and stay true to who you are and what matters most to you. If your family is a priority for you, for instance, but your goal requires you to spend more time away from them, don't neglect them completely. Be determined to make the most of the time you do spend with your spouse and children, and try to carve out more time in your schedule for family activities.

Notice the effects of your determination and be aware if someone or something is suffering as a result, since I'm certain that wouldn't be your intention. Give the things that matter to you the attention they deserve, or they could create a greater challenge for you down the road.

"In order to really enjoy a dog, one doesn't merely try to train him to be semihuman. The point of it is to open oneself to the possibility of becoming partly a dog."
— Edward Hoagland

Chapter 2

Time to Teach an Old Dog New Tricks

Learn the behaviors that will guarantee you success.

"When a man's best friend is his dog, that dog has a problem."
— Edward Abbey

While I was writing this book, my husband, my son, and I added a new member to our family: Dee Dee, a Shih Tzu puppy. As new owners quickly find out, puppies don't come trained . . . at all. For example, Dee Dee didn't realize that she needed to do her "business" outside and not on our carpet or wherever else she felt like doing it. We had to train her to go outside.

Our little friend also didn't know that she wasn't supposed to eat my slippers, chew on paper, scratch the walls, dig in the garden, eat the plants, or bite our fingers. She needed to learn not to do any of these things. And telling her *no* once didn't stop her; we had to tell her over and over again.

We humans are very much like puppies. Our optimal time for training is when we're young, but most of us don't learn how to achieve our desires until we're well into adulthood. How many people were shown the most effective methods for reaching goals and overcoming challenges and adversity in their childhood? How many little kids are taught the importance of a positive attitude?

As we get older, we start to realize that there might be more to life than what we're presently experiencing. We begin to connect with our deepest, most heartfelt passions. We usually haven't learned how to pursue our dreams yet, so we must train ourselves with new disciplines, which takes time. Just like dogs, we're creatures of habit—we'll continue to do the things we've always done, the way we've always done them, unless we're instructed to do otherwise and get lots of practice using the new technique.

What's interesting is that training a puppy in the early stages can be relatively quick, depending on your own commitment to the training and the animal's temperament. But if you bring an older dog into your home, this process can take considerably longer.

Several years ago, my parents rescued an older Lhasa Apso named Heidi. Sadly, Heidi had been neglected, so my mom and dad had to teach her to be housebroken. This wasn't an easy task, but they were highly motivated and didn't give up. After a period of time—longer than they would have liked—my parents succeeded in training Heidi.

At the time of this writing, Heidi is 14, which is "old age" for a small dog. My mother recently told me that the dog is reverting to her old behavior, doing her business on the floor inside my parents' home. Mom said, "It's like training her all over again!"

We humans sometimes revert to our old behaviors and have to train ourselves again. It's hard to imagine why we would ever go back to our old self-limiting ways, yet we occasionally do just that. Therefore, we must replace old habits with new ones and train ourselves to succeed. We can also think of it as building the muscles of discipline: just as we work to tone and strengthen the physical muscles in our body, we have to constantly "go to the gym" to build up our behavior muscles. If we don't, we'll get flabby and fall back into our old state of poor conditioning.

In the past, whenever I've visited an obedience school or a puppy-training academy, I couldn't help but think of the similarities to continuing education for people. It's true that it's best to learn positive behavior at a young age, just like a puppy does; however, we don't always receive the best instruction when we're in our youth. As a result, we may have to commit ourselves to an obedience school of personal growth as adults.

How Can You Teach Yourself New Tricks?

Answer the following questions in a notebook or on a sheet of paper:

1. What skills, attributes, disciplines, and characteristics do I need to develop and strengthen in order to achieve what I want from life?

2. Where will I get the knowledge to do this?

3. What can I do to develop these skills?

Doing your research may take considerable time, creativity, and resourcefulness. Search the Internet, the library, and bookstores; talk to people about what you're seeking and ask if they know anyone who can guide you; find a mentor; and check out community resources such as those geared toward small businesses or senior citizens. You may also want to take workshops or classes or use self-help books to encourage you to discover what you already possess that can help you achieve your goals. Return to the diaries you wrote when you were a child or teenager and rediscover your forgotten dreams, passions, skills, and talents. What you're doing is important work, so give it the effort it deserves.

Anyone Can Learn

My belief is that we need to go to school for the rest of our lives, but now we must attend class at the college of personal growth. This facility is always open, and the enrollment is available to anyone who chooses to enter. The only prerequisite is desire—and when you add determination to that desire, acquiring and applying knowledge will be much easier.

Now, the next step is to determine how you'll learn the discipline that will help you succeed. If you're sure you won't be able to do this, think again. Remember, dogs don't doubt their ability to do something new! If you believe that you can't, you won't even try, and this attitude will hold you back from achieving what you want. Feelings such as *I'm too old to change now* are limiting and will create barriers so that you actually won't absorb new things. If you have this belief, I strongly urge you to erase it from your mind and replace it with a positive, supportive one, such as *I can learn anything when I try to do so,* or *I learn whatever I need in order to achieve my goals.* Have faith in yourself, and commit yourself to learning the new tricks of success.

When I decided to write a book, I didn't have any formal education or experience as an author, and I believed that you had to be a journalist, have a degree in creative writing, or have some other credentials to achieve this aim. I decided to erase that belief, pursue my dream, and write from my heart. In the process, I received guidance from a few highly regarded people in the publishing industry, and I applied myself to the writing task. I discovered that, in fact, I could manifest my dream and was blessed with talented editors who helped me along the way. By being open to my own skills and the possibility that people could assist me in achieving my goal, I was able to overcome any obstacles in my way.

Maybe Guidance and Information Are All You Need

Does your dog ever tilt his head while you're talking to him? I believe this means that he doesn't understand what you're saying. I've never had a dog tell me otherwise!

When *you're* confused, it may mean that you need to sniff out the answers or gather more information. Instead of allowing confusion to paralyze you, allow it to move you to find whatever you need to achieve the clarity you require.

Gaining clarity can be achieved in a number of ways, but asking questions is one of the best methods for doing so. Be certain to pose your questions to the source (or sources) who's most qualified to provide you with the information you need. For example, if you want to open a business, you could ask for advice from your friends who have never run one because you want them to be supportive, but you may not get the answers you need. Also, you open yourself up to hearing their own concerns about financial risks or about "stepping out," or whatever advice they can give you might be colored by their fears. Always consider the source when you try to gather facts and support!

It may be better to track down someone who's actually done what you're aiming to do and achieved success—even if you don't know him or her. Keep in mind that while this may make you slightly uncomfortable, it can be very valuable to use your network to find what you're looking for. You never know who might know someone who can assist you.

And don't be afraid to approach strangers for their help. I've often been pleasantly surprised to see that most successful people are very willing to offer their wisdom and support to others. As I started and grew my own business, I asked for and received guidance from many, many people; even now, I continue to seek advice and insight from other professionals, which helps me grow my business further.

When your dog chews your remote control or gets into the garbage and spreads it across the floor, maybe he's telling you that he hasn't received the guidance he needs! Like our canine friends, we humans sometimes act destructively and need to be reminded to change behavioral patterns that aren't working.

You may not realize that by constantly downplaying your dream—even if you're doing so because you want others to think you're polite and humble or because you're embarrassed—you're enforcing the belief that dreaming big is arrogant, and this is very destructive. Maybe all the guidance you need is to listen to your heart instead of ignoring it out of the fear that people won't like or accept you if you pursue what you want from life. Stop telling yourself, *I should think small, not big* or *Who am I to achieve such a big dream?* You deserve to have all that you desire.

What do you need to know in order to move forward toward your goals? What are the disciplines you need to develop in order to succeed? Discover the answers to these questions, and commit yourself to learning and applying what you've found. Invest the time and energy to research the knowledge that will lead you on the right path and be most beneficial in achieving your goals, and you'll never go wrong!

Financial Services and Retirement Planning

© 1998 Randy Glasbergen
www.glasbergen.com

"Right now I only have three bones, but I figure I'll need at least 750,000 bones when I retire."

Chapter 3

DON'T CHASE YOUR TAIL

Stop doing things that get you nowhere.

"A dog teaches a boy fidelity, perseverance, and to turn around three times before lying down."
— Robert Benchley

Why do dogs chase their tails? I don't believe there's a compelling reason for this, except that they don't realize what they're doing. Human beings are similar, and I know that because I've been there. No, I wasn't spinning in circles trying to bite my back pocket—I was doing things that got me nowhere, but I didn't realize it at the time.

And why do dogs turn around three times before they sit down? I was curious about this behavior, so

I went looking for the answer by reading numerous books on canine history. Apparently, our furry friends turn around three times before they sit or lie down because they're preparing their beds. Dogs actually descend from the wolf family, which lived in the wild and slept on branches and leaves. By turning around several times before lying down, wolves were able to tamp down the branches and leaves to create a more comfortable resting area.

For a dog, chasing his tail serves no purpose. Turning around three times before lying down might have come in handy in ancient times, but no longer. After all, indoor dog beds are not usually made of branches and leaves.

We humans can learn from these two examples. First, we need to notice the things we do that waste time and get us nowhere. Second, we must recognize if we're doing things that may have served a purpose in the past but aren't helping us in meeting our goals today. If we notice ourselves doing them, we need to stop right away.

Barking Up the Wrong Tree

You may be familiar with *insanity* being defined as "doing the same thing over and over and expecting a

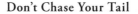

different result." If your activities or behavior aren't producing the results you desire, evaluate them for effectiveness—and if they don't add any value, stop doing them.

This reminds me of the story a friend of mine shared about her dog, Nellie, a playful Border collie. Although Nellie wasn't an old dog, she exhibited the characteristics of senility. For example, whenever a guest arrived at my friend's home and rang the doorbell at the front of the house, Nellie ran to the back door (where there wasn't a doorbell), barked, and wagged her tail. Every time that doorbell rang, Nellie would bark and hurry to the back door, thinking that's where someone was arriving, yet the guest always entered through the front. It never did register with Nellie that the sound of the bell ringing indicated someone was about to enter at the front of the house. She simply didn't notice this pattern.

In addition, Nellie had a housemate, a Persian cat named Baby who loved to climb trees. Fortunately for Baby, my friend's yard was full of them. Nellie often chased Baby around the yard until the cat got bored and scrambled up one of the trees. Nellie would stand at the base of the tree, head stretched up, and bark. Sometimes she did this even though Baby wasn't in the tree, which made her owners laugh. Who knows why Nellie barked at the tree? Maybe there was a bird up there or she thought that Baby had climbed up . . . or maybe she was just engaging in the same old habit.

We humans often behave just like Nellie. In my career, I've chased a lead or pursued a contact only to discover, after a tremendous amount of work, that he or she wasn't the right person to work with in the first place, and I wasted my time barking up the wrong tree.

If you're engaging in similar behavior, maybe it's not a conscious choice. You might not be thinking of other possibilities, or perhaps you find it easier and more comfortable to do the same old thing rather than risk trying something new. You could start at the beginning of a learning curve and make some mistakes, or people around you may be unsupportive of the changes you're making, but it's important to be willing to stop the insanity and engage in more productive behaviors.

Instead of barking up the wrong tree, Nellie could have looked around and possibly found Baby sitting in the *right* tree. This is what happened to me when I looked at the other contacts I had and ended up finding the perfect one. A small shift in my focus, which opened me up to possibilities I hadn't considered before, made a world of difference.

The Pain of Poor Choices

Our puppy, Dee Dee, loves to chase her ball. We'll throw it, she'll run after it and bring it back to us, and we'll repeat this process many times. Sometimes Dee Dee thinks that the ball is under the sofa, when in fact it's rolled into the next room. She'll keep trying to get under the sofa rather than consider what her own eyes have already shown her: that the path to her goal is through the door, not under the couch. My family laughs at the entertainment value of watching a dog think it's on target when it's very far off the mark, but human beings do the same thing. We get fixated on one destination, even though it's a dead end. If we shift our direction by a fraction of a degree, though, we'd recognize a better way and take it.

If we don't recognize the results of our unproductive actions, we may waste time and even experience pain. When Dee Dee was really little, she loved to bite on electrical cords. If she'd continued this habit, it could have led to extreme pain or even death, so she had to learn to refrain from doing so. Similarly, we humans need to notice that if we keep doing some things that don't appear to affect us now, we could get very hurt at a later date.

What electrical cords are *you* biting? Are you risking your health by engaging in bad habits? Are you risking losing your marriage because you're taking your spouse for granted, being unappreciative and neglectful? If so, you need to quit it now.

Discover the behaviors that are preventing you from achieving your goal and may even be taking you in the opposite direction. This awareness will give you the wisdom to change or stop the behavior that's unproductive and may even be harmful. As you move forward, heighten your awareness and continue to notice and reject these self-destructive habits that keep you chasing your tail.

"I'm advertising my new business on the Web. For $25 an hour, I'll come to your house, lick your face, listen intently, wag my tail and be your best friend."

Chapter 4

ONLY INGEST THINGS THAT ARE GOOD FOR YOU

Poisons sabotage success.

"Ever notice that a dog only has two faces? The one you love, and the one you get as it sits and looks at you while it pees on your freshly washed floor!"
— Melanie Rogers

Have you ever seen a dog consume something that wasn't good for him? Take our neighbor's otherwise well-fed pooch, Mack, for instance. He loves to eat insects, and it's not pleasant to watch. Mack weighs only three pounds, and some of the bugs he goes after are about half his size. I don't think the nutritional value of the insects is worth the effect they have on his system, particularly since he often gets very sick in the process. But does Mack stop? No. He still insists on eating them.

Similarly, our dog, Dee Dee, used to attempt to chow down on everything she could get ahold of— she'd go into our garden, grab some bark chips with her mouth, chew them, and try to swallow them. Because she was a puppy, she didn't realize that she shouldn't do that. Fortunately, we knew better, and we'd stop her before she swallowed something that might not feel too good coming out the other end.

Our canine friends aren't always aware of what's good for them. And while we humans do have the ability to know what's good for us, we may not be *aware* that we know. In our state of unawareness, we ingest harmful things, bringing them into our bodies and minds.

One type of poison we take in comes in the form of toxins present in foods and beverages. When speaking to audiences, I often ask, "If I put poison in your water, would you drink it?" What do you suppose is the answer? Obviously, "No!" Unfortunately, we don't tend to think about what we eat and drink in this way, so we ingest these toxic substances without thinking and suffer the consequences. We end up becoming run-down and ill, thus sabotaging our success.

Our body requires good nutrition to survive, as does our mind. If we don't treat our body well, it will respond accordingly. About 25 years ago, I heard someone say, "Most people are digging their graves with their mouths." We may think that one sugary food or beverage a day isn't hurting us . . . until we add up the 365 unhealthy items that we ate or drank this year and calculate the possible damage we've done to our body.

Another toxin we take in regularly is negativity, which also sabotages success. Even a fleeting thought such as *I'm not worthy of achieving my goals* can be lethal, for it leads to another negative thought and another, until we create so much harmful emotional energy that we stop ourselves from moving forward.

The thoughts you have today *will* affect your results tomorrow. In fact, everything you have in your life today is the result of what went into your mind in the past. What do you suppose is the result of telling yourself over and over again that you're crazy for going after your dream? You've turned down the volume on your confidence, enthusiasm, and joy; and the increased noise of your damaging feelings and beliefs has held you back from your goal.

Your negative thoughts and emotions have a lot of destructive energy to be sure, but your positive thoughts and emotions are just as powerful. So why choose to think or feel negatively when you can think or feel positively? You always have the choice to consciously switch out of negativity whenever you experience it—and doing so will help you manifest your dream.

Take a moment now to think about how you choose to feed your body, your mind, and even your soul on a daily basis. Are you consistently eating nutritious foods? Do you drink enough water? Since there's so much evidence about the relationship between diet and moods, I recommend that you become nutritionally conscious and apply healthy eating habits to your everyday life.

In addition, continually fortify your mind with positive thoughts and by speaking positive words. And remember to nourish your soul, which you can do by meditating or reading inspirational books.

Practicing healthy habits and behaviors will foster health in your mind, body, and soul and allow you to live the way you were meant to: with a sense of joy and fulfillment.

"Don't worry—I'm just practicing my Yoga!"

Chapter 5

BE A LITTLE DOG WITH A BIG-DOG ATTITUDE

Your attitude is the little thing that makes a big difference.

*"What counts is not necessarily the size of the dog
in the fight; it's the size of the fight in the dog."*
— Dwight D. Eisenhower

What does it mean to be a little dog with a big-dog attitude?

Little dogs don't realize that they're little; they act as if they're big despite their size. They have no fear and aren't intimidated by larger creatures. Small pooches will try to do things that even bigger hounds might think are impossible. They don't know that what they're attempting is supposed to be impossible, so they try anyway. What a great attitude to walk around with: one that's courageous and confident!

Do you have such an attitude? If not, I strongly urge you to develop one immediately because it's especially good for helping you to hold on to your dream like a dog with a bone. You can connect with your courage and confidence by simply turning up the volume on any positive emotion—they'll flow once you start to feel joy, tranquility, gratitude, or even creativity because all positive emotions enhance each other.

When you add optimism and positivity on top of your determination never to take your eyes off the prize, you'll reduce and possibly eliminate most negative feelings. Frustration and stress will begin to disappear as you focus on fostering more confidence, courage, happiness, and enthusiasm.

Having an intense negative attitude, on the other hand, will stop you in your tracks and send you in a backward direction at an accelerated rate. Such an attitude can start small—perhaps sparked by irritation with the weather, the economy, or some other condition outside of your control—but it will grow and infect all areas of your life unless you stop, consider the ramifications, and change your thinking.

When you maintain a positive attitude, life is far more enjoyable, you'll navigate obstacles better, you'll strive harder and reach higher, and you'll attract to you all that you need in order to achieve your goals.

"Can Do" Keaton

The following story comes from Deneen, a dog handler and trainer. Her canine companion, Keaton, was enrolled in "agility training," a sport that includes leaping over a variety of jumps, tipping a seesaw, zipping through a configuration of upright poles, negotiating a narrow dogwalk, and zooming through tunnels. Here's what this little dog can teach us about having a big-dog attitude:

> When I tell people that I do agility with my dog, they ask, "What breed is he?" and expect to hear "golden retriever," "Jack Russell," or "Border collie." Well, it comes as quite a shock to them that Keaton is a two-year-old, brindle-and-white English bulldog.
>
> That's when the negative comments start: "A bulldog in agility?" "Bulldogs can't do that!" "He could never jump or climb the A-frame!" and "Bulldogs are stubborn, stupid, and not trainable!"
>
> The sad thing was that at first I started to believe them, but Keaton convinced me otherwise.

After my dog's first beginner classes, it became very clear that the A-frame was going to be a monumental challenge, since its peak was 5'6" off the ground. This mountain of boards, with only small slats of wood for traction, started to look a lot like Mount Everest!

On Keaton's first attempt, our goal wasn't the same as that of the other dogs—we simply wanted to have him place his front feet on the frame. We accomplished that aim, and Keaton was rewarded to let him know that he'd succeeded. The next goal was to get all four feet on the frame at the same time. He did it! We offered Keaton another treat and words of encouragement for his accomplishment.

That was all for the first class. I couldn't help but think, *Well, that went well, but it didn't seem to be much of an accomplishment compared to what the other dogs were doing.*

The following week, it seemed that the pressure was really on. The other dogs were sailing up and over the frame on their first attempt, while Keaton was only willing to put a paw or two on the first step.

"That's good enough for this class," the instructor stated. "We'll try for a little more next week."

And that's when more negativity crept into my head. I thought, *Maybe he can't do this . . . he is a bulldog, after all.*

Feeling disappointed, I clipped on his lead and started to follow the others out of class. Suddenly,

Keaton let out a bark and started to pull me, with great determination, back in the direction of the A-frame. Before I could think, *You won't do this . . . you're a bulldog,* he picked up speed, confidently put his feet on the yellow frame, and powered himself up and over it with great ease. Once he was down the other side, he sauntered proudly toward the door as if to say, "So there! We can go home now."

It didn't matter that no one in the class had seen him do it; his confidence and determination filled me with inspiration. We were ready to show everyone what a bulldog can do, and that's exactly what he did at the very next class.

Today, Keaton still loves training in agility and obedience and is preparing to compete for his novice titles. He is a confirmation champion. In his spare time, he plays the piano (yes, the piano), and we are working on a freestyle dance routine.

The lesson my dog taught me is to discard negative thoughts and opinions that others may have and that I've adopted, which have held me back from achieving my goals. He taught me not to worry about what everyone else is doing, but rather to decide for myself what my objectives are and work toward them step-by-step. I learned to plan my strategy and overcome obstacles, and I discovered that I can achieve what seems impossible.

Even if your situation isn't ideal and your circumstances aren't the most opportune, or if you don't believe that you can make huge leaps of advancement in a short period of time, you can be like Keaton and pursue your dream anyway. You may have to place one paw out there at a time, but soon you'll take another step . . . and then another . . . until you'll finally be over the top of your obstacles and well on your way to achieving your goal.

Remember that your attitude will greatly affect your outcome—so an optimistic, positive one will turn the impossible into the possible.

Trust Yourself

It's important to note that being positive and optimistic does not mean being arrogant. It's totally unattractive to see people running around being braggadocios or shouting about how important they are. All attitudes are held within and will be expressed externally without your having to work at communicating them verbally. People will sense your confidence naturally, and if you're truly secure, you won't need constant reassurance from others that you're all that you say you are.

In fact, if you investigated the characteristics of some of the most successful men and women in the world, you'd find that they give very little energy or concern to what others think of them. (Terry Cole-Whittaker wrote a wonderful book on this subject called *What You Think of Me Is None of My Business*.)

Don't be concerned with what others believe or say about you, especially when they start to see the wonderful transformations that are taking place in your life. Change is sometimes difficult for people to adjust to, and when an individual starts to change for the better, those around him or her often respond negatively. Don't let others' inability to handle your success dissuade you—instead, focus on your goal, maintain your positive attitude, and build your faith. After these folks start to see your level of commitment and notice that the changes are positive, they'll be happy for you if they truly do care for you.

Know that achieving great success and accomplishments requires an attitude of faith, confidence, and assuredness. Create a deep sense of knowing that you have infinite potential and believe in yourself. Develop a winner's state of mind, that inner knowing that you've already arrived at where you truly desire to go. Walk around as if you're already there, feeling what it's like to have accomplished your goal and live the life of your dreams, being the person you've always wanted to be and sharing your gifts with others. You can do this by reciting affirmations that help you create these feelings and by using your imagination to create in your mind the scenario you want for yourself.

Emotions have tremendous power to attract to us what we desire, so turn up the volume on your confidence and watch the amazing results!

© 1999 Randy Glasbergen
www.glasbergen.com

"This is so cool! I'm barking at a cat in Australia!"

Chapter 6

WHEN YOU FEEL YOU'VE REACHED THE END OF YOUR LEASH, GO FARTHER

How to handle adversity and overcome any challenge.

"Every dog has his day."
— Miguel de Cervantes

The first day we brought Dee Dee home, I put on her brand-new beautiful collar, clipped on the matching leash, and prepared to go for a wonderful morning stroll, just as I'd seen so many of my neighbors do with their dogs. If you're a dog lover, you may already know where this is going, but I truly had great expectations of enjoying a peaceful walk with my new pal.

If you've ever attempted to take a puppy for his first walk, you know that he'll want nothing to do with a leash. His instinct is to run in whatever direction strikes his fancy, in the pursuit of total freedom. For the first few weeks, I experienced exactly that whenever I tried to walk Dee Dee—just like any other puppy, all she wanted to do was sprint, dash, and run in circles.

Since dogs aren't allowed to run free in most societies, we must teach our canine friends to follow our lead and not pull on (or avoid) the leash. Training puppies to go only as far as the leash will allow is fairly simple, because if they try to go any farther, they'll choke themselves and become very uncomfortable. We humans experience a similar result when we try to stretch beyond our limitations: because we're easily trained not to stretch ourselves too far, we tend to blindly accept those limitations.

The confines of your comfort zone are set by your beliefs, which were probably created at a young age. Your parents may have told you, "You can't do that!" or "You'll hurt yourself!" and at that precise moment, you set a boundary for yourself; that is, you determined the length of your leash.

It's also quite possible that over the years you gradually shortened the length of that leash out of fear. Perhaps someone told you that you had limitations and you believed them, without even exploring whether or not that was true. Fear of discomfort and uncertainty will keep you at your current comfort level and on a short leash. However, while it may seem that others set your limits, you're in charge of your own life, so you're the one who chooses how long your leash is.

The length of a leash represents the restrictions you place upon yourself. Whenever you say, "I can't take it anymore. This is as far as I can go!" these are clear statements of defeat or resolve that reflect an intention to hold yourself back and no longer move forward. You must remember that if your leash isn't long enough to allow you to achieve your goals, you can get a longer one or an adjustable one. In other words, if an old belief is holding you back, you've got to get rid of it, revise it, replace it with a different belief, or let go of it altogether and run freely in the direction of your goals.

I believe that, like a puppy, you're meant to pursue ultimate freedom and act without limitations. Of course, limitations can play a beneficial role in your life, but you need to ascertain if they're making you safe or weighing you down. For example, if you've experienced abuse and are saying, "I can't take it anymore," I highly recommend sticking to that decision. However, if you're uttering that phrase because you have a defeatist attitude and you're not experiencing any physical or psychological harm, then I recommend that you pull at that leash and stretch yourself a bit more. You could be extremely close to getting the results you want.

You may also just need to take a rest and replenish your store of energy. You might feel as if you're at the end of your tether, but maybe you only need a break. Perhaps you just need to take time, reflect, notice what you're feeling, and become aware of what's holding you back. Once you take that break, you may then be ready to charge forward past any obstacles.

Pet stores sell leashes that allow you to push a button for the lead to release or retract. The first time I used one of these, I thought of how some people live their lives on a short leash, not realizing that they have the power to push a button and allow themselves to go much farther. They've chosen how far they're going to go, and although they have an opportunity to go beyond that, they don't bother to expand their lives or the length of their leash. Occasionally, they may pull beyond their lead in an attempt to reach something outside of their normal limits, but when difficulties arise, they tend to draw in and shorten it back up.

It's likely that you will only ever attempt to go as far as you believe you can go, but when you expand your beliefs, you expand your reach. You may think that you've "reached the end" of your rope, but there may be more of it available. Have you decided where your rope ends? Think about your self-imposed limits for a moment—are they holding you back from achieving your goals? What would happen if you chose to let go of these limitations?

Build Faith

If you're still looking for answers and feel that you're at the end of your leash, engage some additional patience and start to build up your faith. Faith is a state of being, a feeling of inner knowing, a conviction that you absolutely will achieve your goal. Faith is energy—a mighty and powerful force. You're going to need that energy to continue on the path to achieving your goals, and it's easily found within you. Like determination, faith is something you can choose to have or not have. It's up to you.

You can build faith by using your imagination and creative thoughts to "act as if" you have what you desire. Essentially, you think about your ideal outcome and imagine what it will feel like to reach it. While you fully engage your imagination, you start to experience the sensation connected with the scenario you're creating in your mind. The emotion is generated by this imagined experience, even though you're simply pretending. Once you've seen your desired outcome in your mind's eye and know what that feels like, you can practice experiencing that sense of accomplishment.

"Acting as if" takes practice and may seem uncomfortable at first. You'll have to consciously reject any negative thoughts that pop up, such as *This is silly; This won't work;* or *This feels nice, but it can't really happen.* With repeated practice, you'll master the art of creating faith as well as the other powerful emotions you need in order to reach your goals. Just start with a little bit, notice what it feels like, and add more to it. Add a little more faith every day until you reach a point of absolute certainty.

Keep in mind that having faith will result in the unknown becoming known. In other words, when you've decided on an outcome, even if you don't know how you're going to achieve it, having faith will allow the answers to be revealed to you. Trust in this powerful energy—the results will simply astound you.

"First my ball rolled under the sofa, then my water dish was too warm, then the squeaker broke on my rubber pork chop. *I've had a horrible day and I'm totally stressed out!!!*"

Chapter 7

DROOL UNTO OTHERS AS YOU WOULD HAVE THEM DROOL UNTO YOU

The most important lesson you can learn.

*"The average dog is a nicer person
than the average person."*
— Andy Rooney

We are all one! This is one of the most powerful and profound phrases known to humankind. Because we are indeed all one, it's also true that what we do for others, we do for ourselves.

If you think that being nasty to just one person won't hurt you, I suggest you think again. There's a natural law of the universe that clearly states: "What you put out, you get back." So if you're putting out bitterness, hostility, anger, resentment, or any other negative emotion, it will be returned to you. Any thought, negative *or* positive, will come back to you. Once you create the energy of that thought or feeling, you send it into the universe, and the universe only knows how to respond in kind.

This is why my friend Mark Victor Hansen taught me to "be nice to everyone!"—not just to some, but to all. Each of us needs to become unconditionally giving and caring, sending out love without an expectation of having it returned to us. Yes, it will return, but it won't necessarily be in the form we expect it to be in or arrive when we expect it to. Similarly, if we're being respectful, respect will be returned to us. If we're being kind, kindness will be returned to us, and so on. It may not be returned from whom it was given to, or we might have to wait a long time for the respect to return to us; nonetheless, it will be returned.

Unconditional Love on Four Paws

When my Shih Tzu, Dee Dee, was a small puppy, she'd go everywhere with me (at least wherever she'd be welcomed). I even brought her to meetings with Fernando Martinez, my Website designer, who warmly and openly accepted her. She was such an adorable puppy that she attracted people to her like a magnet.

One day as I was sitting in the reception area of Fernando's building, a gentleman walked out of one of the other offices and came up to see my little Dee Dee. While he didn't tell me his name, he did share a story about one of his dogs. It seems that he'd owned a beautiful Scottish terrier he loved dearly, but at the young age of three, she'd died of cancer. He and his wife missed their dog terribly, and she convinced him to go to the local humane society to see if there was one they might want to adopt. They found another Scottie who was about two years old, yet nobody seemed to want her because she was rather unattractive and was missing hair around one ear. Yet the man and his wife felt so sorry for the dog that they adopted her.

A few years later, this homely Scottish terrier woke up the couple in the middle of the night to warn them that their house was on fire. Their Scottie saved their lives, just as they'd saved hers. I was struck by this powerful illustration of the universe returning to the couple what they'd given out.

Without a doubt, dogs embody unconditional love. Your canine companion will love you no matter what kind of day you're having. Even if you're sad, she'll be there for you. When you're frustrated, depressed, and drained, feeling unable to give to anyone, she'll wag her tail and lick your face. She won't determine how she's going to treat you based on your mood—she cherishes you regardless.

I think that this type of love is one of the reasons why people love their pooches so much. I find it interesting that those who have pets adore them without any expectation of love in return, but they don't apply this same sentiment to other human beings. Our relationships would improve significantly if we adapted the same high level of acceptance and warmth with each other that we offer our furry friends.

Most men and women are afraid of being hurt, rejected, or disappointed, while dogs are not. And unlike us, dogs don't hold grudges or dredge up the past and fret over it. Of course, if they've been traumatized, they'll remember that trauma. I know a woman who adopted a mixed Lab and Border collie who'd been rescued from the Gulf region of the United States after Hurricane Katrina. The dog, whom she named Jack, would become very hyper and anxious anytime he heard thunder, and he suffered such severe separation anxiety when she'd leave him to go to work that he'd tear the house apart. This woman ended up giving Jack to a friend who worked out of her home and was able to take him with her just about every place she went. Clearly, the poor thing remembered the trauma he'd suffered. But, like other animals, he didn't remember if his owner had been irritable a few hours earlier or had scolded him last week. Do you think we could learn from this forgive-and-forget behavior? You bet we can.

Don't Bite the Hand That Feeds You

When my family's two puppies were very young, they'd playfully bite our fingers. My son, Michel, would teasingly say to them, "Don't bite the hand that feeds you."

The "hand that feeds you" may be your customers, your employer, your life partner, your children, your other family members, your friends, or even strangers. The word *feed* could also be replaced by the word *love*. The hand represents the whole person. And the word *bite* could be replaced by the phrase *be nasty to*. So this phrase could also be said as, "Don't be nasty to the person who loves you."

Being nice to everyone and being uncondition- ally loving, without expectations of having that love returned to you, also means being respectful of oth- ers. Respect is too often overlooked when it should be

57

high on our values list. There have been times in my own career when certain individuals have treated me inappropriately, only to show up at my office later to look for a job. How do you think I felt about them at the time? Do you think their previous treatment had any effect on my decision to hire them? Since we just never know where people will show up in our lives, being nice to everyone and respecting them in spite of any differences we may have is vitally important.

Of course most of us don't mean to be nasty or cruel, but too often, we act that way without thinking. Because we're stressed out, we snap at those we work or live with, and then we're too embarrassed to apologize. And when we're the ones whose feelings have been hurt, we plot revenge instead of exploring why we allowed ourselves to become upset by someone's behavior. No one can make us feel angry, sad, or frustrated—we create these emotions in ourselves when we choose to respond to challenging situations by telling ourselves that we're victims of circumstance.

What we can do instead is choose positive feelings such as curiosity, which helps us explore why we're so sensitive to a particular comment or why the other person is acting in a way that appears to be cruel. Learning from the experience, using the opportunity to better understand ourselves and others, is always

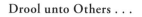

much better than creating a cloud of negativity.

Again, we must remember the all-important rule: *Drool unto others as you would have them drool unto you.* It's priceless advice!

© 2000 Randy Glasbergen
www.glasbergen.com

"Remember the Golden Rule: Drool unto others
as you would have them drool unto you!"

Chapter 8

COME ON OUT OF THE DOGHOUSE

Courageously step forward into growth.

....

"Be very careful what you set your heart upon, for you will surely have it."
— Ralph Waldo Emerson

Is it really a "dog eat dog" world out there? Have you become backed into a corner, convinced that there's no way out? Maybe you took an action that backfired or experienced an event that left you thinking you have no options. Feeling trapped causes a sense of desperation—now that you've been backed into that corner, you may feel as if vicious beasts are awaiting you. Is it possible that you can come out without provoking an attack? Perhaps your fear will disappear when you face it. What if you emerged from your corner and were greeted by a friendly dog with a wagging tail instead of a scary monster?

While life can sometimes be "ruff," there's no need to cower in the comfort of your doghouse. Come on out and face the world! Hiding won't solve anything; it could quite possibly make matters worse. Pretending that unpleasant realities aren't there doesn't make them go away. If you have something you need to face, then do so head-on. Whatever your dilemma is, there's always a way to solve it and resolve the situation gracefully. Making the choice to forgive yourself and others could be the solution. You might need to learn from the experience and forgive yourself for how you've acted, or you may need to stop blaming another person. Whatever is required, find a way to resolve your problems rather than sneaking off to the doghouse and hoping they go away.

If somebody did something that resulted in your becoming seriously upset, however, your best approach may be to just let the sleeping dog lie. You might not be able to come to a resolution if the other person is clearly unwilling to make peace with you, and you certainly don't want to give in to the temptation to retaliate. Consider actively choosing to leave the problem behind you and moving on.

Windows of Opportunity

When you've decided to courageously step forward and achieve your goal, you'll start to find windows of opportunity opening up for you. But you won't see them if you're not willing and ready to do so.

My neighbor's dog, Holly, asks to go outside by walking up to the door and waiting patiently for her owner, Cheryl, to open it. When Cheryl does open the door, the dog moves to the side and sits down. Cheryl smiles as Holly sits there . . . still inside. Holly looks at the open door and then looks back up at Cheryl. She waits until my neighbor is just about to close the door, and then she runs outside. Cheryl calls this "Holly's window of opportunity," and she always takes advantage of it—but at her own pace.

This behavior reminds me of people who see their own windows of opportunity and don't do anything until they're about to close, and then they dash forward and go for it. But what about those who have windows of opportunity open up for them and don't do anything at all? Or worse, the windows are there but they don't even see them?

Every day provides new opportunities, and you need to be ready to seize them. Sometimes the best ones are right under your nose, but if you don't have windows of opportunity or can't find them, you must create them wherever you can.

As a child, I was sheltered from the planet's tragedies, and once I started to hear about them through the media, school, or friends, I was shocked to learn that in some places on Earth, people were starving to death! How could that be? I'd thought everyone had a happy family, a comfortable home, plenty of food to eat, and clean clothes on their backs.

With this new knowledge, I couldn't go back to the way I used to see the world. Since life wasn't what I'd imagined it to be, I decided that I didn't want to grow up! As I became increasingly aware of all of the realities of life and started to face more challenges, I often longed to step back into the comfort I'd known in childhood.

I came to learn, however, that life has one constant, and that is change. Change is inevitable—everything in the universe is in the process of transformation. You know, as I do, that we don't have control over everything that's happening *around* us, but what we can control is the way we respond to what happens *to* us. Our response determines our results.

If the change that's happening in your life is not something you've chosen, ignoring it won't help matters. The good news is that when you do find the courage to face change, you may discover that it's a window of opportunity that's just waiting for you to climb through it. There have been times in my own life when a dreaded or forced change resulted in one of the best growing and learning experiences of my life. Getting divorced was a very painful experience for me, for instance, but as I look back now, I can honestly say it made me grow tremendously.

You choose how you'll respond to events and what you will do about them. With a positive attitude and a courageous approach, you'll be able to navigate through change more effectively and minimize any suffering. If the change is going to happen, or is happening anyway, you may as well look at it as your window of opportunity and make the best of it.

"*Cats*—the fragrance for dogs who dare to be different!"

Chapter 9

DOG INSTINCTS

Trust your inner knowing.

....

"Outside of a dog, a book is man's best friend.
Inside of a dog, it's too dark to read."
— Groucho Marx

Dogs have incredibly refined instincts: they can perceive danger and will growl when they feel that it's near, and they know whether a human being is loving or not. One of the reasons for this is that canines' ability to detect odor is perhaps a million times more acute than ours is. It's speculated that certain diseases such as cancer, epilepsy, and tuberculosis emit a distinctive smell that's recognizable to dogs, so they have a keen awareness of when someone is ill or about to become so. There are numerous stories of people who suffer from epileptic seizures whose dogs notify them prior to the onset of an episode so that they can place themselves in a safe position and get the medication they need.

Our furry friends unquestioningly trust that what they're sensing is accurate. My cousin Fern shared this story about a Schnauzer named Zeus and the other dogs whose instincts about him turned out to be right on the money:

> Zeus had cancer when I met him, with a tumor the size of a tennis ball on his back leg. My German shepherd, Duchess, as well as other dogs, instinctively knew not to play with him, to respect him and his illness. It amazed me to see that the animals intuitively knew not to disturb this Schnauzer.
>
> Zeus's owner took him to Boston for cancer treatment, and when they returned, the dog appeared to be healthy. He was no longer limping and was even running around again. The dogs began to play with him and include him in their roughhousing. But then nine months later, they started to leave Zeus alone again even though he appeared to be fine. Zeus's owner noticed this and decided to take him to the veterinarian. The vet determined that the Schnauzer's cancer had returned, and he died shortly thereafter.

How amazing that because of the dogs' keen instincts about danger and sickness, they were able to detect Zeus's health issues even before his owner did.

My Aunt Betty told me a similar story about a pooch owned by her cousin Neil, who was a wireless air gunner for the Royal Canadian Air Force (RCAF) during World War II. Neil was very attached to his dog, whom he left with his mother, Jessie, while he was overseas fighting. One night, Neil's dog woke up and started to howl for no apparent reason. He did this for hours, and no matter what Jessie did, she could not settle the dog down. Within a few days, the RCAF notified Jessie that her son had gone missing a few nights earlier after not returning from his mission, and he was now presumed dead.

How did Neil's dog know that he was killed on that particular night, when they were thousands of miles apart and an ocean separated them? The only answer is: a dog's instincts.

Randy Chartrand is an expert in dog psychology and one of the best trainers in Canada. As he says, "Dogs are emotional. Fear is a survival emotion—an emotion that will save a dog's life. Sometimes it's better for dogs to take off when they sense danger, and they will do just that."

We humans are emotional as well. Since we can detect danger, we'll feel fearful when we sense that we're under threat. But we also have so many destructive, self-induced emotions cluttering our instinctual senses that we become confused.

One of the best things we can do to get in touch with our instincts is to become quiet and listen to our inner voice. If we discover that our instincts are fear based, we can then evaluate whether that fear is real or imaginary. Most of the time, what terrifies us is rooted in our imagination; we're afraid of what *could* happen rather than what's actually happening.

Just as with dogs, your fear can be a survival mechanism. When you feel afraid, you need to get in touch with that emotion and determine the cause—if there's validity to it, this awareness can help you determine your course of action. Most important, you must take that action. If you need to, go ahead and do as a dog would do and take off when you sense danger. Or if you discover that your fear is rooted in your imagination, step forward and face it, and then watch it vanish right in front of you.

Learn to trust your instincts, for they can be the greatest barometers you have. Once you begin to do so, you'll be able to easily determine if a certain feeling is coming from your inner knowing or from *f*alse *e*vidence that only *a*ppears to be *r*eal; that is, from *fear*. If you want to know what your instincts are communicating to you, do the "gut" test, because it will never lie. So ask yourself, "What do I feel is true in my gut?"

When you learn to listen to your gut and trust your instincts, you'll begin to build keener senses and be better equipped to sniff out trouble and avoid it. This will allow you to make decisions based on an accurate reading of the situation, rather than giving in to fear or anxiety.

*"The greatest pleasure of a dog is that you may make
a fool of yourself with him and not only will he not
scold you, but he will make a fool of himself too."*
— Samuel Butler

Chapter 10

BARK FOR WHAT YOU WANT

Don't keep quiet about your needs and desires.

....

"The silent dog is the first to bite."
— German proverb

Jack Canfield taught me many years ago that we should ask for what we want. We ought to be like my little Dee Dee, who will walk over to her human friends, lie down on her back, and look at them as if to say, "Please rub my tummy!" She will lie there trustingly, gazing up with her big brown eyes, and wait confidently for someone to rub her tummy.

Do dogs think twice before they ask for what they want? They'll ask to be let outside; they'll ask to be fed; they'll ask you to play ball—they'll look up at you with those puppy-dog eyes and you're doomed. Pooches don't analyze what they want; they just go for it. They're not even afraid to be told no, because they'll simply keep trying.

We humans need to remember to ask for what we want, appropriately and respectfully. (We may even want to consider using our own puppy-dog eyes as we do so!) Yet why is it that we're more inclined to go to strangers for favors instead of our own friends and family members? It seems that we don't ask our loved ones for things because we're concerned that if we do, we'll jeopardize the relationship. But if people who love each other can't do things for each other, who can they do them for? Those who care about us would love to help us out . . . but since they don't have crystal balls, they need to be asked.

I believe that when human beings give each other a hand, this creates a chain reaction of giving. So we must open ourselves up to allowing others to recognize our desires instead of pretending that we really don't care whether or not our requests are fulfilled. Too often we mistakenly assume that if we get what we want, someone else will have to sacrifice, yet this may not be the case.

Don't overlook the fact that when you allow other people to help you, they then feel needed. When you're open to asking for and receiving assistance, you'll find that most folks love to help because it gives them pleasure to know they can do so. Accept what they're offering and you will, in turn, be giving *them* a gift. And when you're on the receiving end of a request, try to oblige. Help others in any way you can. In fact, don't wait to be asked—if you see someone struggling and you know you can assist them, do so. Give without expectation of anything in return; otherwise, you may only set yourself up for disappointment.

If you can't come to the aid of others, don't feel bad about yourself. Be honest with those who are asking for assistance and communicate positive feelings of love, faith, and creativity. Sometimes the best thing you can do for them is to simply lend a sympathetic ear. Other times, you may be able to make suggestions as to where these folks might be able to get the assistance they need.

For example, a friend of mine felt bad that she couldn't help a pal who was dealing with the pressing needs of an aging parent, but she did know of a woman who performed companion care for people in this situation. The companion turned out to be a lifesaver for the woman and her elderly parent, and she was very grateful to our mutual friend for the suggestion.

Bark Gently and Respectfully

As you've probably learned when someone has ordered you to do something, making demands leads to resistance, not results. So if you happen to come across a person who's using a harsh tone to make a request, recognize that his bark is probably worse than his bite. This individual could be experiencing challenges in another area of his life, and his frustration is coming through in the tone of his voice. Keep in mind that his tone may have nothing to do with you.

The same thing may happen if you're the one who's asking for help. If the other person gets upset with you, it's most likely because of her own problems. She may be feeling overwhelmed and respond to your request with anger, resentment, or frustration. If this is the case, don't take it personally. *There's nothing wrong with asking for help.* Have compassion for your frazzled friend who's too upset to enjoy the pleasure of giving to another right now, and look for someone else to assist you.

When you make a request, it's best to do so with sincerity, honesty, and openness. Be clear on what you want, and just ask for it—don't be intimidated, or fearful of a negative response. Your emotions will come through in your request, so if you're timid, those you're

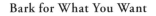
asking will pick up on that and may feel uncomfortable about responding. Be confident and assured. After all, what's the worst that can happen? If they say no, you haven't lost a thing.

You may want to consider making your request in another way by providing more information. In sales school, I was taught that "the sale begins when the customer says no!" In my training, I also recall learning that negative responses simply mean that customers need more information to rid themselves of their resistance. Try to find another way to make the request—if you continue to do so in a way that shows you're passionate, respectful, and thoughtful of others, perhaps the law of averages will work for you. Perhaps you won't get a favorable response on your first or second request, but eventually you just might get the answer you're looking for.

Bark for what you want, but do so gently and respectfully and with your big puppy-dog eyes. You'll be irresistible!

"The microphone is so you can go to
Internet chat rooms and bark at strangers."

Chapter 11

WAG YOUR TAIL

Be happy and show appreciation.

> *"Pet a dog where he can't scratch*
> *and he'll always be your friend."*
> — Orville Mars

How often do we show our gratitude and appreciation to others? Too often when we have the urge to do so, we become reluctant—perhaps we're afraid to admit that we're vulnerable and needy at times or we're embarrassed about getting "sentimental." I know that it took me a long time to realize that I needed to express appreciation more often, and I had to get used to doing it.

Human beings may not have learned how to be thankful or appreciative when we were growing up, and now it feels uncomfortable or strange to say, "Thank you" or "You're a great friend and I really treasure you." Dogs, on the other hand, express appreciation all the time. Have you ever been greeted by your pooch when you've been out for a while? As soon as she spots you, her behavior lets you know just how happy she is to see you.

Contrast this with the countless times you've walked in the door after a long day at work to find your family members so busy that they didn't even notice you'd arrived. If you've only been gone for five minutes, your dog will give you a warm reception, licking you and even jumping up with enthusiasm, because your mere presence makes her jubilant.

As your dog proves to you on a daily basis, showing appreciation to others benefits them *and* you. The act not only makes them feel good, it does the same for you as well. That's why it's said that it's better to give than to receive: it's a known fact that helping others will make you feel even more wonderful than you do when you receive aid.

You can give a gift to other people by expressing your appreciation, whether it's for something as simple as being who they are or to honor the special things they've done for you. You might thank them for being positive and encouraging to you when you were feeling pessimistic, or you might acknowledge their small acts of thoughtfulness. Or maybe you could just wag your tail when they come home.

Make Wagging Your Tail Part of Every Day

Both dogs and humans crave affection and attention, and both would rather have *negative* attention than none at all. Since we're all social animals and want to feel connected, when dogs and humans feel neglected, we'll instinctively do something to gain attention, and what we do may not be positive.

In puppy training, owners are taught to praise their pups when they do something they're being taught to do, because this reinforces good behavior. Remembering how wonderful it feels to be rewarded, the puppy will repeat the behavior. This principle of acknowledging good behavior works with humans, too. Praise others when they display positive behavior and you'll see them repeat it.

Feeling appreciated is as wonderful as having someone tell you they care for you. Appreciation communicates gratitude, admiration, thankfulness, and respect—feelings that are universally loved. Since you know how nice it feels to receive, find ways in which you can show your appreciation to your family members, customers, co-workers, employer, neighbors, friends, and even strangers.

Remember that expressing your gratitude and appreciation to others will increase your own level of happiness. When you feel good, you express joy, and when you express joy, you feel good—this creates a circle of love. Giving unconditional thanks and appreciation is a caring gesture that will release the powerful energy of love, and it will be returned to you many times over. Imagine what your life would be like if you created a powerful circle of love and appreciation. . . . Start right this second to find someone, or many people, to whom you can express your genuine appreciation and gratitude. And keep wagging your tail every day!

"My therapy is quite simple: I wag my tail and lick
your face until you feel good about yourself again."

Chapter 12

KEEP YOUR NOSE WET

What to do when you're feeling "ruff."

....

*"A dog is the only thing on earth that
loves you more than you love yourself."*
— Josh Billings

Have you ever witnessed people push themselves
way beyond their physical limitations and risk their
health in pursuit of a goal? It amazes me when men
and women invest so much of themselves—time,
energy, and money—in becoming successful. In the
process, they sacrifice the very thing that will allow
them to enjoy this new level of achievement: their
wellness.

Like humans, dogs have been known to push themselves beyond their physical limits, too. As you may recall, I introduced Max, a Scottie with the dogged determination to play, earlier in the book. Here's another anecdote about this dog from his owner, David:

> When we lived in Boston, two girls from the neighborhood would take our two dogs out and walk them and play with them, in order to give them some exercise. The girls would have the dogs chase a ball across the floor in their basement, and Max would do this until his paws bled—and still go back for more. Max was determined to keep going in spite of the pain he felt.

Although we can learn from the little Scottie's example in his determination to play, we can also learn from his refusal to give up in the face of pain. Was it necessary for Max to play so hard that his paws bled? No! Unfortunately, he was so determined and fixed on his goal that he pushed himself far beyond his physical limits.

Having determination doesn't mean that we go beyond our physical limits to the point of discomfort. We need to remember not to push ourselves too far—working long hours, not eating properly, not drinking enough water, and not exercising are all signs that we've done just that. When we realize that we're engaging in such harmful behaviors, we need to immediately stop and look after ourselves.

Notice when you start to feel the effects of working too hard, for instance, and adjust before you create an even greater health risk. Your wellness should be a high priority for you, since creating phenomenal success is of no value if you're not healthy enough to enjoy it. You must take care of your body because it's the vehicle that will carry you to your goals.

When a dog's nose is wet and cool, it usually means that he's healthy. If his nose is dry and warm, it tends to indicate that there's something wrong and attention is required. Are you ignoring a dry and warm nose? Do you have physical symptoms that you've been dismissing as unimportant? If so, you must notice them, address them, and ask yourself if you've been neglecting your health.

What do you do to stay well? And what do you do to return to that wellness when you do become ill? While you're striving to reach your goals, there are probably going to be days when you don't feel your best physically, mentally, or emotionally. You'll need to turn up the intensity on your positive attitude on days like this and maybe even exert a little more energy.

You may have heard this saying: "A professional is at his best, regardless." What this means is that while you may not always feel terrific, you should perform at the best of your ability in the moment. It's also important to notice when you aren't feeling well and address it rather than hope it goes away on its own.

The mind-body connection is a powerful one. If you're angry or depressed, it will probably show up in your body as fatigue, stomach problems, tight muscles, and so on. If your physical health is suffering, it will be harder for you to feel joyful and buoyant or to keep the positive, alert attitude that can propel you forward toward your goals. As you can see, it's vital that you pay attention to how you feel and address your physical, mental, and emotional health.

Shake Off the Negativity and Take Time to Play

Dogs don't appear to worry. Luckily for them, they don't have the painful side effects of this pointless mental exercise: digestive issues, high blood pressure, headaches, and so forth. Many people, on the other hand, do have a tendency to worry, creating anxious thoughts and fear. Worry causes intense pain and self-destruction, so it should be avoided, but it can also be a helpful sign that you're in danger. Rather than ignoring feelings of worry, think of them as signals that you should tread cautiously: become curious, ask questions about the situation, and be careful. However, don't engage in worry as a habit, since it can create psychosomatic disease as well as prevent you from feeling a sense of well-being and optimism.

It may help you to keep in mind that when dogs get out of the water, they shake their bodies to dry off. Think of this action when you're feeling an increased level of negativity such as anxiety, stress, anger, or frustration. Why not shake it off as if it were merely water? Negativity has no purpose in your life and needs to be removed immediately—shaking it off will foster your physical, mental, and emotional health.

Also, do be sure that you have plenty of playtime in your life, since it's so good for the mind, body, and soul. Pooches never forget to play, but you probably do, especially when you're pursuing your goals. Now, being like a dog with a bone does *not* mean you should refuse to take time for fun. You'll actually be more efficient and clearheaded if you create balance in your life by having time to play and relieve your stress and worry.

Studies show that after a vacation, people are more focused, alert, and productive. Don't wait until you're completely frazzled to indulge in playfulness—make it a part of your everyday life.

Practice Proper Grooming

Our canine friends need to be groomed not just to look good, but to keep them healthy, too. A matted, dirty coat can cause skin problems and discomfort, while regular brushing can actually help a dog feel healthy, invigorated, and loved.

Proper grooming is important for you, too. For good or bad, people will judge you based on how you look even before you've opened your mouth. If the impression you give them is that you don't care very much about your body, they'll get the message that you aren't someone who's worthy of being nurtured or treated with love and respect. Would you trust your money or your hard work to a project overseen by someone who spends no energy on taking care of himself or making a good, professional presentation? Or would you rather invest in someone whose appearance shows that he values himself and the impression he makes?

Take regular trips to the "groomer" and keep up on your health tests, physical exercise, and appearance. You'll feel much better if you do.

> *"No one appreciates the very special*
> *genius of your conversation as a dog does."*
> — Christopher Morley

🦴   🦴   🦴

Chapter 13

THE DOGMA OF SUCCESS

The inside scoop on how to live your life.

"To his dog, every man is Napoleon;
hence the constant popularity of dogs."
— Aldous Huxley

There are those who work like a dog to make things happen, those who watch things happen, and those who wonder what happened. Obviously, you'll want to be the person who makes things happen.

Sometimes you just have to work like a dog. If you want to be extraordinary, you must do the things that ordinary people aren't willing to do. Success doesn't occur through merely wishing for it, nor does it occur through force. Trying to coerce success or getting incredibly frustrated when things aren't going exactly the way you'd like them to demonstrates an unawareness of the perfection of the universe.

When my dog, Dee Dee, wants to go out, she'll stand by the door and look at me with those puppy-dog eyes. She trusts that if she stands there, I'll notice and take her out. It may not happen the moment she gets to the door, but she trusts that it *will* happen. She may get impatient and bark after a while, but she knows that I'll eventually come and take her for a walk.

After Dee Dee and I get outside, she may tug at her leash to go in one direction when I want her to go in another, but she does follow my lead without a struggle—she isn't attached to walking a particular path around the block. Dogs know that wherever they go, they'll find a nice spot to do their business and something interesting to sniff out, whereas we humans try to dictate how and when everything will happen. We get impatient quickly, and we start trying to control others and take charge of every detail of the situation instead of simply trusting that what needs to occur will do so in due time.

All things are happening for a reason, and if you attempt to understand why everything is happening as it's happening, or try to analyze why they've happened the way they have, you may become frustrated. Sometimes it's necessary to let go, or, as the famous saying goes, "Let go and let God." But letting go and letting God doesn't mean that you can sit back and wish for things to happen without doing anything about it. On the contrary; you have a responsibility for what's going to show up for you in your life.

To create success, you need to align all of the factors for it in a fashion that will produce your desired results—not the results someone else wanted for you, but what you truly want for yourself. What are those factors? Depending on the outcome you're seeking, you'll create your own formula based on what you want to produce. However, you'll need some fundamental ingredients such as passion, integrity, determination, focus, optimism, faith, a positive attitude, awareness, intention, commitment, and love.

All dogs and all humans are unique: just as there's no single training program that will work for all canines, there isn't one that will work for all humans. To discover the best training method for your pooch, you have to understand her individuality. Similarly, for you to bring out the best in yourself, you need to understand your unique set of behaviors, habits, desires, talents, and needs.

What do you tend to focus on? What are your priorities? How do you operate most efficiently—do you work best alone or in a group, in the morning or in the evening, at a desk or in a situation where you can move around? Becoming acutely aware of who you are can help you recognize what you're creating in your life and discover which methods will let you make the most of your gifts so you can transform your goals into concrete manifestations.

If you want to be successful, it's also a good idea to find someone who already is and follow him or her around like a puppy. Success breeds success, so modeling another person's achievement will significantly reduce the amount of time it takes to reach your goals. A role model has already been there, learned the lessons, and discovered what to do—and more important, what *not* to do. Follow this individual's example, but tailor it to yourself because you're a unique person with your own goals. Then look for ways to improve these techniques for achieving success.

When I launched my first online e-mail campaign, for instance, I got in touch with some people who were getting the results that I wanted. I asked them how they achieved their success and listened intently as they told me about the things they did that were "results producing" and the things they did that turned out to be "learning experiences." I adapted their experiences to my plan, eliminating the possibility of costly mistakes, and created ways to improve my own campaign to generate increased sales for my business.

Unlimited Potential

Just like our furry friends, human beings are far more capable than we currently appear to be. Do you realize that service dogs can do things such as turn on lights, push buttons, pull books out of backpacks, get pens out, and help folks navigate a wheelchair lift? Until I started studying canines more in depth, I had no idea that they were capable of performing all of these actions once properly trained.

We can also be trained to do things we might have thought were impossible. The only thing that stops us is our limiting beliefs about our own abilities. If we believe that we won't be able to do a certain thing, then that's exactly what will happen. However, if we choose to adopt the philosophy of "there is a way— and I will find it," then we move beyond the impossible to the possible.

You've got the ability to do anything you want with your life, as long as you're willing to let go of your attachment to exactly how and when your dreams will become reality. Know that; trust it and be committed to your goals, and don't let anyone or anything stand in your way or try to take your dream away from you. As Winston Churchill is said to have instructed, "Never, ever, ever give up" on it.

Be clear about your dream. Then be the dog with a bone, have faith, and know in your heart that your dream will manifest!

> *"My only goal in life is to grow up to be*
> *the person that my dog thinks I am."*
> — Unknown

Chapter 14

Lap Up Your Success

Take a big bite out of life.

"Just give me a comfortable couch, a dog, a good book, and a woman. Then if you can get the dog to go some-where and read the book, I might have a little fun."
— Groucho Marx

"Paws" for a moment and give thanks for the many blessings in your life. Paws and take inventory of the great gifts you've been given and are about to receive, as well as the ones you share with others. Paws to note how your gratitude creates a wondrous feeling of joy.

As you're on your journey to success, do remember to enjoy the trip. Stick your head out of the car window, just like a dog does, and let the wind blow through your hair.

This journey requires your commitment. Just as the successful people you know have chosen to be this way, you can also choose to be successful. Since you're continuously evolving and transforming, you can decide how you'll grow and make positive progress every day, in every way.

Once you've got a dog-with-a-bone attitude, keep it. Hang on to that dream of yours and don't let anyone try to take it away from you. Remind yourself of what keeps your jaws clenched on that bone. This is your inspiration. This is your fire. This is the one thing that will help you hold on to your dream when it seems much easier to let go of it.

The universe lines up to provide for a person who's a dog with a bone: miracles start to happen and "serendipitous" moments occur. When you open yourself up to possibilities, you'll discover the resources and methods for lapping up your success and fully enjoying your life.

And don't forget to give yourself a treat when you've reached a goal—or even just taken one step toward its achievement! Dog owners give their pooches treats as rewards, and you should do the same for yourself in order to stay motivated and feeling great.

Finally, celebrate! Celebrate your life, your learning, your every success. Celebrate your accomplishments, big or small. And celebrate the success of your friends, colleagues, and family members. Enjoy your wonderful and exciting journey. Unlike cats, you only have one life to live, so do so to its fullest. Take a big bite out of life and savor every mouthwatering moment!

© 2001 Randy Glasbergen
www.glasbergen.com

"We'd like tonight to be special.
Could you get some water from the toilet
and put it in a champagne bottle?"

Acknowledgments

Thank you to my wonderful son, Michel, for your wisdom and insight to include humor and stories in this book. I love your unconditional love for animals, especially dogs . . . there are actually so many things I truly love about you that words on a page could never express them fully.

To my husband, Denis, thank you for being completely loving and devoted.

With a heart filled with gratitude, thank you, Mom and Dad, for your unconditional love and loyalty and for bringing dogs into my life.

My grandmother Alva McColl passed away many years ago, yet I'm grateful for her devotion to dogs. She was recognized as the world's first dog psychologist; she was the editor of *Dogs in Canada* and the first female president of the Canadian Kennel Club; and she was an award-winning journalist and a sought-after dog judge. I'm grateful for the gift of dog wisdom that she brought to the lives of thousands of others.

My greatest challenge in completing this book was the effort it took to keep the acknowledgments at a reasonable length. It was tremendously difficult to limit my thanks because of the overwhelming amount of help and support that many people—colleagues, friends, and complete strangers—so generously provided to complete, enhance, complement, and improve upon the ideas and messages of this book. To you all, I'm grateful. Thank you.

A big "woof" of thanks to all of the dogs who generously, unconditionally, and willingly teach us humans some extremely valuable life lessons.

🦴 🦴 🦴

About the Author

Peggy McColl is an internationally recognized expert in the area of destiny achievement whose purpose is to make a positive contribution to the lives of millions of others. She's been inspiring individuals, experts, professional athletes, and organizations to reach their potential for the past 25 years. She is the president and founder of Dynamic Destinies Inc., an organization committed to delivering sound principles for creating lasting and positive change.

Peggy lives in Quebec, Canada, with her son, Michel, and her husband, Denis. You can contact her at: **peggy@destinies.com** or through her Website: **www.destinies.com**.

Notes

Notes

We hope you enjoyed this Hay House book. If you'd like to receive a free catalog featuring additional Hay House books and products, or if you'd like information about the Hay Foundation, please contact:

Hay House, Inc.
P.O. Box 5100
Carlsbad, CA 92018-5100

(760) 431-7695 or **(800) 654-5126**
(760) 431-6948 (fax) or **(800) 650-5115 (fax)**
www.hayhouse.com® • **www.hayfoundation.org**

Published and distributed in Australia by: Hay House Australia Pty. Ltd., 18/36 Ralph St., Alexandria NSW 2015 • *Phone:* 612-9669-4299 *Fax:* 612-9669-4144 • www.hayhouse.com.au

Published and distributed in the United Kingdom by: Hay House UK, Ltd., 292B Kensal Rd., London W10 5BE • *Phone:* 44-20-8962-1230 *Fax:* 44-20-8962-1239 • www.hayhouse.co.uk

Published and distributed in the Republic of South Africa by: Hay House SA (Pty), Ltd., P.O. Box 990, Witkoppen 2068 • *Phone/Fax:* 27-11-467-8904 • orders@psdprom.co.za • www.hayhouse.co.za

Published in India by: Hay House Publishers India, Muskaan Complex, Plot No. 3, B-2, Vasant Kunj, New Delhi 110 070 • *Phone:* 91-11-4176-1620 *Fax:* 91-11-4176-1630 • www.hayhouse.co.in

Distributed in Canada by: Raincoast, 9050 Shaughnessy St., Vancouver, B.C. V6P 6E5 • *Phone:* (604) 323-7100 *Fax:* (604) 323-2600 • www.raincoast.com

Tune in to **HayHouseRadio.com®** for the best in inspirational talk radio featuring top Hay House authors! And, sign up via the Hay House USA Website to receive the Hay House online newsletter and stay informed about what's going on with your favorite authors. You'll receive bimonthly announcements about Discounts and Offers, Special Events, Product Highlights, Free Excerpts, Giveaways, and more! **www.hayhouse.com®**

HAY HOUSE

Tune in to Hay House Radio to listen to your favorite authors: **HayHouseRadio.com**®

Yes, I'd like to receive:

☐ **a Hay House catalog**
☐ *The Christiane Northrup Newsletter*
☐ *The Louise Hay Newsletter*
☐ *The Sylvia Browne Newsletter*

Name_____

Address_____

City_____ State_____ Zip_____

E-mail_____

Also, please send:

To:

☐ **a Hay House catalog**
☐ *The Christiane Northrup Newsletter*
☐ *The Louise Hay Newsletter*
☐ *The Sylvia Browne Newsletter*

Name_____

Address_____

City_____ State_____ Zip_____

E-mail_____

If you'd like to receive a catalog of Hay House books and products, or a free copy of one or more of our authors' newsletters, please visit **www.hayhouse.com**® or detach and mail this reply card.

To:

HAY HOUSE, INC.
P.O. Box 5100
Carlsbad, CA 92018-5100